Lynne,
Thank you
for connecting
fondly
Beth Totten

Connections

POETRY BY
Elizabeth Totten

PHOTOGRAPHY BY
Jake Totten

FIRST EDITION

E-mail: liztot@yahoo.com

@connectionspoetryphotography

@connections_poetry_photography

Book design by Mel Chapman Designs

Connections is dedicated to Mary Kathryn McGuirk Palmer.
You always knew that I would publish one day.
Mom, I only wish you were still with us to share these moments.

Table Of Contents

Author Notes

Have you ever thought of someone and suddenly the phone rings and it is that person? Or, have you ever thought of a song and then heard that song played and replayed during your day? There are also times when a television commercial or a movie may remind you of something that happened earlier in life. Often, the little things that seem so insignificant are the events and experiences that bind us together. Through these scenarios we find caring, support, strength and love.

We are connected…to our family, friends, and others in our universe. We are connected to nature and the world. We are connected to spiritual, environmental, historical and political environments around us. Our interconnectedness helps to develop us into the beings that we are. This book of poetry and photography was created to explore that connectedness.

We worked on this book from different places and different perspectives…Jake was in Maine and Beth was in New York. With his photographer's eye, Jake took pictures that he thought were interesting and shared them with Beth. Beth wrote poetry inspired from the photographs. Additionally, Beth wrote poetry and sent those to Jake who, in turn, would take pictures inspired by the poems. This was an interesting project for both mother and son and through this work, their personal connection has grown stronger.

Synchronicity

Coincidence, God Winks, Connections,
Meeting in this place,
Dotting the lines from point A to B
And finding that our routes correspond.

Understanding that we were meant to meet
Like passengers on the same bus
Or birds on the same flight south
Exactly at this time in life.

Comparing days- Not like dressing alike but
Instead when we found the starfish.
You, at Cape Cod.
I, in Myrtle Beach.

Or when we both lost our last surviving parent
Within the same week in May
Orphaned in our mid-years
Yet, joined together on this journey.

Sharing profound sorrow
And finding new joys.
We are connected here
One to another.

Lazy Summer

Lazy summer afternoon strolls-
Through meadows,
Through woods.

Meandering through life-
Surviving dreams,
Surviving awakenings.

Walking into the light-
Smiling thoughtfully,
Smiling peacefully.

Walking towards the horizon-
Outstretched arms,
Outstretched heart.

Mother's Perfume

The sweet smell transported me
To dark loamy soil and a rust eaten shovel,
Mounding dirt loosely around small seeds
Then nurturing them all summer.

The sweet smell took me
To eating fast food delicacies and
Giggling as the pop bubbles
Tickled our noses.

The sweet smell took me
To date nights for you and Dad.
I would secretly tiptoe to your room
And stand, inhaling that fragrance.

The sweet smell took me
To late night snacks in the kitchen
Talking and laughing,
While everyone else dreamed.

The sweet smell took me
To Sundays, when the simple act
of worshipping as a family
fortified us for another week.

The sweet smell of your perfume
Called to me and I followed it-
All through the grocery store,
Until the fragrance was lost.

The Telephone Call

She called again last night.
"Hello" "Hello" "Who's there?"
"Is anyone there?" I ask.
"Good-bye" she whispered after a minute or two.

A crank call, a prank.
She calls at least once a week,
Sometimes more often.
Her voice is soft, sultry.

I wonder who she is.
I wonder where she is.
I wonder why she calls.
I wonder if she dialed with intention.

Perhaps she is alone
And the call is an attempt
To reach out to someone
-- Anyone at all.

She's retired, a widow,
Or confined to a bed
And not able to even get to a window
To look outside or see another.

She could be lonely
And she calls my number
Because she has the need
To hear a friendly or familiar voice.

After a call, I wonder if it was
A wrong number dialed in haste…
She didn't mean to dial my number
So merely wished me a pleasant "good-bye."

But sometimes I have the distinct feeling
That she is someone I know or knew-
Someone who just needed to hear my voice again
to let me know she is still thinking of me.

Foundation

Our roots delve
Into the dark loamy earth
Entwining ancestral memories.

Our heritage built
Upon porous, slippery granite
Strengthening fragile muscles.

Our journey bolstered
With brown, rusted leaves
Cushioning bludgeoned spirits.

Our foundation settled
On sweet, spongy moss
Nourishing unspoken dreams.

Broadcast

You told them
EVERYTHING
About my day,
About my thoughts,
About my feelings.

You broadcast my thoughts
The way a farmer sows his seeds,
Scattering them
For all your world to see.

You told me
NOTHING
About your day,
About your thoughts,
About your feelings.

My secrets shared
To unknown souls.
Your secrets shrouded
From inquiring minds.

This is not a relationship.
This is not a commitment.
This is not loyalty.
This is not the way
I want to live.

Circles

You tucked me
Into bed safely,
Then lingered
Til sleep came.

You carried me
Over steep hills
When I couldn't
Get there alone.

You held me
On strong shoulders,
Towering high above
To watch life's parade.

You taught me
To drive carefully
Through life
Efficiently caring for all.

Much Later,

I nourished you
With a favorite meal
Of meat and potatoes
Served piping hot.

I held your hand
As we drove to
Learn your medical needs
As time ran short.

I regaled you
With remembered stories
Of childhood pasts while we
Laughed and cried together.

I tucked you
Into bed softly
Then lingered
Til you left us.

Brave Spores

Brave spores,
under the woodland canopy,
gently falling to the beat
of the winged birds,
find fertile residence.

Intricate fronds,
unearthed in the spring,
swaying to the rhythm
of the gentle breeze,
discover the sun.

Long silky stalks,
in the loamy earth,
thrive here
a testament
to enjoy and endure.

Spring Arrives

My eyes glistened and overflowed,
much as the rain misting the fields
earlier in the day.

I could see spring
in the small purple
crocus adorning my front yard.

The sweet scent of
flowers, grass and newness
Left me giddy with joy.

Chickadees, sparrows and robins
gobbled the suet and seed
from the feeders.

Blue Jays cawed their warnings
reminding smaller birds
to steer clear of their perch.

My hand rested gently
on the old screened door
I pushed it into Spring.

Pathways

Hands are the pathway
To truly knowing a person.
They can be expressive, tentative
Bold and helpful.

I remember a maiden great aunt,
Grey hair, gnarled hands
Hemming dresses and trousers.
Clothing a community.

I see my mother's hands working,
Soft, gentle and constantly moving.
Kneeding dough, brushing hair
And praying the rosary daily.

Age shows in my hands
In the crevassed blue veins,
In the crooked fingers.
Arthritis beginning now.

I find comfort in hands,
Caressing loved ones,
Wiping away tears,
Encouraging strength with a touch.

In Hand

He found you
Broken, weary,
On cold, hard dirt
A damaged wing?
A fall from a nest?

His gentleness,
That often heals my heart
From hurt, anger
and horrific fear,
Offered you hope.

Much like the trust
You experienced when
Your bird mother
Fed you from her mouth,
You dwelled in his embrace.

After a short respite,
You flew off,
Changed by the encounter.
Your sweet song flowed.
The moment celebrated.

How I long for...

Sunny blue skies and clouds
fill the day but the cold
has me fleeing for warmth inside.

how I long for the sun
to warm my face,
my arms, my weary bones.

wintry wind whips
and pelts snow on windows.
we've been huddled
inside for far too long.

how I long for spring
for chirping birds,
for bees, for dragonflies.

somber, solemn, quiet
encompasses us for months
and isolation takes a toll.

how I long for others
to whisper, dance or
offer a compassionate touch.

The Fortune Teller

My life can be seen clearly, she said,
As into the tent she strolls.
In just fifteen minutes
She will tell me all that life holds

The aura my body emits is green
She hints the color is hope.
A compassionate hue, she insists,
The color of nature and growth.

The love of my life will be handsome,
Complimenting my talents and skills.
Travel will fill our days
But alas, we may never visit Brazil.

My life's work, she is certain, will be a success
Healthy savings I'll hold secure.
And, the true length of my career?
It is only known I will endure.

My days will be long and fruitful.
There will hardly be time for a breath.
"And, how long will I live?" I wonder.
She smiled. "Life will go on until death."

Buying an Appliance

I'm looking for a machine that will haul
My laundry down to the river and beat it on a rock
Like my momma's momma's momma used to-
Wring the water out with her two gnarly hands.

I'm looking for a machine
I can dance to, like the rhythm
Of laundry is life undressed,
Agitation incantations of a monk from Tibet.

I'm looking for a machine that will love
The scarlet cashmere sweater solemnly
Vowing to honor, care for and cherish it
Long after it has turned salmon.

I'm looking for a machine that will ease
My fear of separation not allowing
The right argyle sock to leave the left for
A thin, monochromatic nylon gigolo.

I'm looking for a machine that will spit
Nickels and dimes from my Tommy Hilfiger jeans
Right into a coin drawer-
Cash register ringing up a sale.

The man told me he's looking for the same
Damn contraption--all he got in stock are Whirlpools
That got no reason, rhythm or respect.
I bought me a nice new shiny one.

Written with a prompt from fellow writer Glenn Miley.

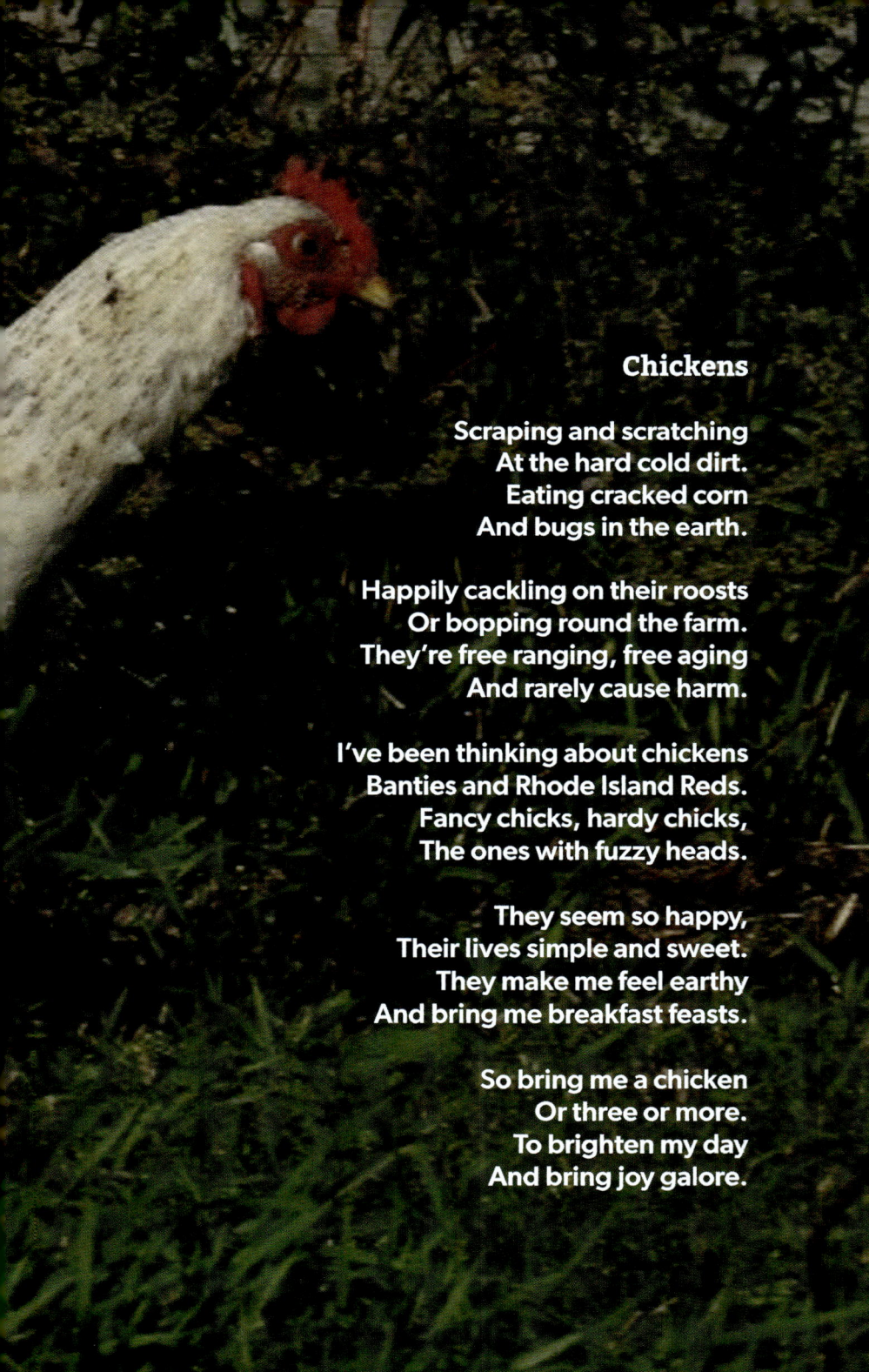

Chickens

Scraping and scratching
At the hard cold dirt.
Eating cracked corn
And bugs in the earth.

Happily cackling on their roosts
Or bopping round the farm.
They're free ranging, free aging
And rarely cause harm.

I've been thinking about chickens
Banties and Rhode Island Reds.
Fancy chicks, hardy chicks,
The ones with fuzzy heads.

They seem so happy,
Their lives simple and sweet.
They make me feel earthy
And bring me breakfast feasts.

So bring me a chicken
Or three or more.
To brighten my day
And bring joy galore.

Today

God,
Help me to see the beauty
And kindness in everything
I experience,
Today and Always.

God,
Help me to realize the problems
Of my brother are
My problems also.
Today and forever.

God,
Help me be joyful
As I look upon the glories
Of nature that surround me.
Today and every day.

God,
Help me to remember your presence
In darkness and sunshine
As you are with me
Today and forever.

Just Be

Be kind.
The world is not a gentle place.
Denial can devastate.
Praise can encourage.

Be patient.
Everyone moves at a different pace.
Anxiety fuels hurt.
Care fuels peace.

Be real.
Imitation is all around us.
Diversity makes us human.
Uniqueness makes us.

Be thankful.
Our life is rich in many ways.
Rudeness complicates.
Gratitude heals.

Healthy

Weave your salad,
Roma and arugula,
Twisting through scarlet berries.
Purple carrots complete it.

Today, our fixings,
Green, red and purple
Selected at a box store.
Garden is a departed friend.

Years before, Grandpa
Planted corn, squash
With beans nearby.
The three native sisters thrived.

Now, my hands in dirt,
Caress and knead
Mix in nutrients.
Warmth fills me again.

I believe in completing
Sudoku in pen.
Puzzles are an adventure
In crisp black ink.

I believe in giving
All you truly have.
It will return to you
at unexpected times.

I believe in gratitude.
Giving thanks stablilizes,
Creating peace and
Community.

I believe in marigolds
And bright red tulips.
Gardens are quite
Contemplative places.

I believe in quietly
Studying a spider's web.
Simple acts help us
Understand others.

I believe in compassion
Every single day.
Kindness multiplies
And refreshes.

Clouds

As children, we made great discoveries
Finding flying boats,
Hearts, dinosaurs and more
Above us in the skies.

Look at the way the clouds drift
Across the blue field.
Their pearly chests
Puffed and proud.

Fast moving, stormy,
Full of precipitation.
They can drown us
In sheets of sorrow.

Slow drifting, peaceful,
Allowing the sun a peek.
Their absence lets the sun warm us
To the depths of our hearts.

Clouds mimic life,
bringing chance meetings,
Hopes and dreams,
In a panoramic array.

Believing

She smiles warmly
And her blue eyes echo a greeting.
A blossoming almost-adult,
she effortlessly lifts
Two pristine boxes from a rack.
Her brightly art-ified sleeve aims
These towards me through the window.
Shafts of persimmon and strawberry colored
Flowers with verdant leaves
Cascade the length of her right arm.
The realness of it is
A reminder that spring
In all its color, buoyancy and resilience
Is the impetus to begin again.
The tangy smell of tomato,
Pepperoni and mozzarella
Waft from the packages
And my thoughts wander
To my garden dripping
With red plump roma fruit.
She smiles warmly
As her blue eyes say farewell.

The Perfect Start

Watch the achromatic liquid
Swirling round the rim of the cup.
The gray day overwhelms us
Until we've consumed this stuff.

The acrid aroma piques
The senses in our mind,
While we stand and determine
Just which will be the kind.

Cold filtered water
And fresh roasted beans,
French pressed, freshly ground,
Italian or Columbian?

It matters not
truth be told.
Just pour one that tastes
brave and bold.

Pour us a cup of that
ink-like brew
No creamer, sweetener
or extract will do.

Let us inhale that liquid
Swirling round the rim.
And start our day
Full of vigor and vim.

New Life

So profound,
one diminutive shoot.
Hopeful, yearning
It reaches arms
to the sun.

Held sacred,
a solitary leaf.
Viable, craving,
It gathers nourishment
in soil.

Renewal

Every so often
We should take time
To inspect and reflect.
We need a spontaneous cleanse,
Purging hate and self-doubt,
Opening the doors to our soul.
We should be beating apathy
from rugs and washing windows for
An honest and clear view of self.
Time to scrape the paint,
Fill the holes,
And smooth the biased roughness.
Sealing ourselves,
With a fresh colorful coat
And the power to effect
Real and lasting change.

First Trip

Skyscrapers above.
People below,
Swarming like insects
Feasting on roadkill.

Central Park Artist
Cartoons your portrait,
Freckles shown as
Large as shiny quarters.

Homeless man
Wheedles coins
From harried
Gucci-festooned tourists.

Wall Street Broker
Patiently waits
For next connection
In New York City.

Depression

She cries every morning
In the shower where no one sees.
Overwhelming sadness over unrealized dreams,
Abandoned relationships and barren possibilities.
In her eyes, each day is
The beginning of massive defeat.
After showering, she practice smiles in the mirror
Watching her reflection for signs of melancholy.
She dresses meticulously for success
And prays today will be better.

Gray

Gray gull
Screeches over
Into the great abyss
To a future unknown.

Weary feet
Trace other footsteps
Through mud and ice
Journeying to work.

Squirrels scamper
Across scaly maple branches
Dancing and jousting.
Laughter fills my head.

My heart
Believes that on
Dark, dank days
We must seek joy.

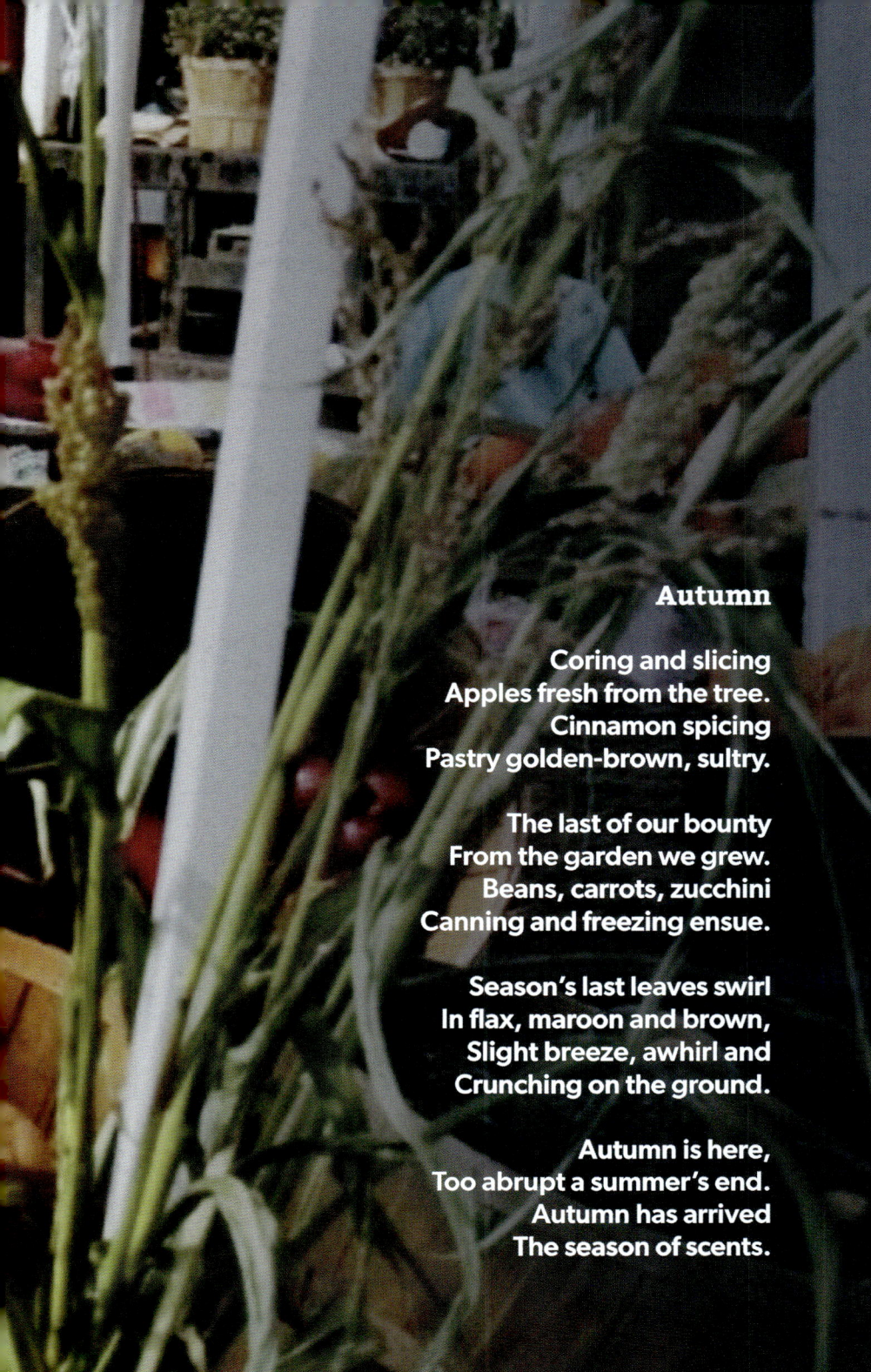

Autumn

Coring and slicing
Apples fresh from the tree.
Cinnamon spicing
Pastry golden-brown, sultry.

The last of our bounty
From the garden we grew.
Beans, carrots, zucchini
Canning and freezing ensue.

Season's last leaves swirl
In flax, maroon and brown,
Slight breeze, awhirl and
Crunching on the ground.

Autumn is here,
Too abrupt a summer's end.
Autumn has arrived
The season of scents.

You Whisper

You whisper
Of crusades
To magical places
Visiting castles, dragons and fairies,
Traveling by caravan.

You whisper
Of journeys
To foreign jungles
Frolicking monkeys, toucans and bugs,
Orienteering overgrown paths.

You whisper
Of trials
And treasures
Greeting vagabonds, farmers and waitresses
Driving country roads.

You whisper
Of the road
And danger
Seeking direction, speed and velocity
Screaming when lost.

I whisper
Of coming home
And resting
With husband, children and friends
Cherishing the welcome.

The Library Book

Dog-eared pages
Burnished with coffee splatter.
Yellowed tape holds life together.
These pages tell tales
Of author and enchanted readers,
Of years catalogued through
Inked and stamped cards
Stuffed into a back pocket.
Spine cracked but not broken
Its journey coming unglued and
Still the story continues.

Wanting

Quiet silence
Is that which I yearn,
To be alone completely,
To be able to breathe
Fresh, clean air
From a mountain or hillside.

Contented peace
Is that which I seek,
To be blissfully happy,
To be able to roam
The savage woods
Without a human companion.

Social kindness
Is what I wish,
To be personally content,
To be able to banish
The ties of society
And find true, caring people.

Dedicated

You sacrificed
For those you love.
Not on an altar
Like a lamb but
With hard work-
With perseverance.
You sheared hours
From your day
To shelter us.
You protected our flock
From hidden enemies.
You harvested, fed, and
Clothed us
With woven fibers of
Gaily knitted sweaters.
You labored
From dusk to dawn,
With love for us.

The Birds

The cardinals and blue jays,
Finches and sparrows,
The barn swallows
Nesting in the upper beams
Of my garage.
We feed them
Seeds and nuts.
We watch them
Grow and struggle.
We identify them
With a 1955 copy
Of Peterson's Field Guide
Tracing their ancestry
Through generations.
They'll leave soon
In the spring,
We'll wait and watch
For their return.

Friendship's Communion

A divine gift
You to me
A sacramental reminder of
The kindness of humanity.

A divine gift
A rite anointed
Through shared memories
And contemplative conversations.

A divine gift
Based on intoned prayer
Shared beliefs
And courageous faith.

Your Waters

When I feel weary,
Your waters cleanse me
Washing sludge
From my life.

When I feel helpless
Your waters soothe me
Drumming methodically
Against my body.

When I feel grief
Your waters surround me
Gently hugging
My anguished self.

When I feel misunderstood,
Your waters comfort me
Reflecting sun
Deep in my soul.

When I feel happy,
Your waters delight me
Playfully lapping
My innermost thoughts.

When I feel love,
Your waters embrace me
Passionately cuddling
My eager heart.

Sleep

Pull the blanket
Over your weariness.
Feel the soft comfort
Envelop you.
Breathe deeply, in and out.
Repeat often.
Smooth the crevices
Of your face, of your mind.
Massage your muscles.
Sleep. Rejuvenate. Reimagine.
Dream of awakening
To a new spring,
For self, for family,
For community
For our world.

Operation Relocation

In the before,
You had free run of the attic.
Scampering across the beams,
Climbing interior walls,
You came a freeman.

In the then,
You examined a wire contraption.
Sniffing peanut butter,
Circling the box,
You entered a captive.

In the now,
You are released to a new forest.
Clambering paths,
Scaling trees,
You are an explorer.

Night

When sleep won't come
numbers barrage my brain,
overheard conversations
repeat and haunt.
Shadows loom large.

As night languishes,
common sense flashes
to forgotten events,
forsaken places and
impending tragedies.
Time is chaos.

In the morning light,
moss catches dew.
Fiddleheads unfurl curls.
Sparrow feeds on spider.
Dawn glows softly on pine.
Night is defeated.

Rebirth

I hold this new life
Close to me
Its warmth fills
My soul.
My depression lifts
And I find that the
Great void inside me
Has been filled.
Life is good.
There is meaning and purpose.
I can live again.

My Friend

You have made me
Smile, frown and wonder.
You have helped me
Enrich myself as a human being.
You have challenged me
To search deeper into my spiritualistic self.
You have questions my beliefs
And listened attentively to my thoughts.
You have helped me to understand
My weaknesses
And strengths.
Thank you.

Winter Blues

Curtains of white
Wash my garage away,
walls of attacking ice
hurling fiercely on this pristine morning.

We wait another five, ten
fifteen minutes,
Solitary figures
watching for a break in the fury.

When white is all you can see
Is that a world devoid of color
Or a panorama of color?
Does anyone really know?

We wait another five, ten
Fifteen days,
Haggard spiritless vagabonds
Watching for change.

We dream of a gardener's palette
Sunny daffodils,
Purple crocus and tulips blazing.
Praying for the resilience of spring.

Portrait of a Lady

Black and white, its edges fading,
her portrait relocated
from attic to basement to office.
Her likeness, once reverently
placed in an ornately carved frame
and displayed proudly in a drawing room.
A full life: she played, loved,
mourned, laughed and cried.
A daughter, sister, wife, aunt, mother.
She is, today, a nameless ancestor.
Although I don't know who she is,
She lived and was a part
of our humanity and our family ancestry.
Her portrait now holds
a special place in our home.

My Prayer to God

Father,
Let me run softly
through meadows
of green grass
and wildflowers.
Let me glide quietly
through the air
like an eagle
in flight.
Let me love tenderly
all of the people
You have given
to me.
Let me die peacefully,
glorifying You
and all of Your
great works.

Published in Oblates Magazine, 1980

A Prayer for Compassion

Help me to open my heart to your peace.
In these hectic, breathless days,
Help me to remember the true reason for my being.

Open my eyes to see the needs of others.
Open my mouth to speak your kindness.
Open my heart to offer your hospitality.
Open my arms to give your love.

Help me to find the right path
In today, in tomorrow.
Help me to clearly see where I need to be.

Open my eyes to see the needs of others.
Open my mouth to speak your kindness.
Open my heart to offer your hospitality.
Open my arms to give your love.

Help me to accept the place where I am
In this time of uncertainty and isolation
Help me to remember you.

Open my eyes to see the needs of others.
Open my mouth to speak your kindness.
Open my heart to offer your hospitality.
Open my arms to give your love.

The Box

Filled to overflowing with
His favorite things.
The blue shirt with the hole
Under the arm
That he never cared about.
The books stacked inside
Waiting to be read
In the quiet of some night.
The baseball he caught
The day he saw Roberto Clemente's
Amazing throw from right field
In the 1971 World Series.
The pocket knife he took
to Boy Scout Camp,

Still well honed
Shining in the sunlight.
A photograph from
A long forgotten vacation
To the lake where we swam
Laughed and loved.
A pair of red converse sneakers
With a gigantic hole where his
Small toe could poke out.
His things
All tossed in a box.
He left them
Without a backward glance.

Special thanks to….

To my husband, Keith and children (Art, Kaite and Jake) who have encouraged me to continue my writing and offered lots of good material for future books!

To Jake for working on this project with me. I'm so proud of the man you are.

To Melanie Chapman for her extraordinary designs. You are a very generous and talented woman.

To the Evening Writing Group at the Canastota Public Library. Your support and critiques are always appreciated.

Each of you motivates me to be a better writer.

To friends and family who asked me for more.